Give your brain a boost with CGP!

Pencils at the ready — this fantastic book from CGP is going to take pupils' Mental Maths skills from zero to hero in no time at all.

It's bursting with activities designed to build those crucial Mental Maths skills, with every single day of the spring term covered.

We also included heaps of helpful examples and engaging pictures to aid pupils along the way. Ideal for use anywhere — at home, in class, on a rollercoaster...

What CGP is all about

Our sole aim here at CGP is to produce the highest quality books — carefully written, immaculately presented and dangerously close to being funny.

Then we work our socks off to get them out to you — at the cheapest possible prices.

Contents

☑ Use the tick boxes to help keep a record of which tests have been attempted.

Week 1
- ☑ Day 1 1
- ☑ Day 2 2
- ☑ Day 3 3
- ☑ Day 4 4
- ☑ Day 5 5

Week 2
- ☑ Day 1 6
- ☑ Day 2 7
- ☑ Day 3 8
- ☑ Day 4 9
- ☑ Day 5 10

Week 3
- ☑ Day 1 11
- ☑ Day 2 12
- ☑ Day 3 13
- ☑ Day 4 14
- ☑ Day 5 15

Week 4
- ☑ Day 1 16
- ☑ Day 2 17
- ☑ Day 3 18
- ☑ Day 4 19
- ☑ Day 5 20

Week 5
- ☑ Day 1 21
- ☑ Day 2 22
- ☑ Day 3 23
- ☑ Day 4 24
- ☑ Day 5 25

Week 6
- ☑ Day 1 26
- ☑ Day 2 27
- ☑ Day 3 28
- ☑ Day 4 29
- ☑ Day 5 30

Week 7
- ☑ Day 1 31
- ☑ Day 2 32
- ☑ Day 3 33
- ☑ Day 4 34
- ☑ Day 5 35

Week 8
- ☑ Day 1 36
- ☑ Day 2 37
- ☑ Day 3 38
- ☑ Day 4 39
- ☑ Day 5 40

Week 9

- ☑ Day 1 41
- ☑ Day 2 42
- ☑ Day 3 43
- ☑ Day 4 44
- ☑ Day 5 45

Week 10

- ☑ Day 1 46
- ☑ Day 2 47
- ☑ Day 3 48
- ☑ Day 4 49
- ☑ Day 5 50

Week 11

- ☑ Day 1 51
- ☑ Day 2 52
- ☑ Day 3 53
- ☑ Day 4 54
- ☑ Day 5 55

Week 12

- ☑ Day 1 56
- ☑ Day 2 57
- ☑ Day 3 58
- ☑ Day 4 59
- ☑ Day 5 60

Answers 61

Published by CGP

ISBN: 978 1 78908 763 5

Editors: Emma Clayton, Eleanor Crabtree, Camilla Sheridan, Hayley Thompson, George Wright

With thanks to Sharon Gulliver and Karen Wells for the proofreading.

With thanks to Emily Smith for the copyright research.

Cover and graphics used throughout the book © www.edu-clips.com
Clipart from Corel®

Coin images used on pages 10, 45, 56 and 61: 5 pence coins © iStock.com/duncan1890, 10 pence coins © iStock.com/john shepherd, 20 pence coins © iStock.com/Jaap2, 2 pence coins © iStock.com/peterspiro, 1 penny coins © iStock.com/coopder1

Printed by Elanders Ltd, Newcastle upon Tyne.
Based on the classic CGP style created by Richard Parsons.

Text, design, layout and original illustrations © Coordination Group Publications Ltd. (CGP) 2021
All rights reserved.

Photocopying this book is not permitted, even if you have a CLA licence.
Extra copies are available from CGP with next day delivery • 0800 1712 712 • www.cgpbooks.co.uk

How to Use this Book

- This book contains 60 daily practice tests.

- We've split them into 12 sections — that's roughly one for each week of the Year 1 spring term.

- Each week is made up of 5 tests, so there's one for every school day of the term (Monday – Friday).

- Each test should take about 10 minutes to complete.

- Pupils should aim to do their working in their heads, without writing it down.

- The tests contain a mix of mental maths topics from Year 1. New Year 1 topics are gradually introduced as you go through the book.

- The tests increase in difficulty as you progress through the term.

- Each test looks something like this:

The Week and the Day of the test are shown at the top of the page.

The instruction the pupil needs to follow is in the box at the top of the page.

There's an example at the top of the page. The correct answer is shown in red. Talk the pupil through the instruction and the example so they know what to do.

There's a score box at the bottom of the test. Use this to keep track of how well the pupil has done.

There are between 4 and 10 questions for the pupil to answer.

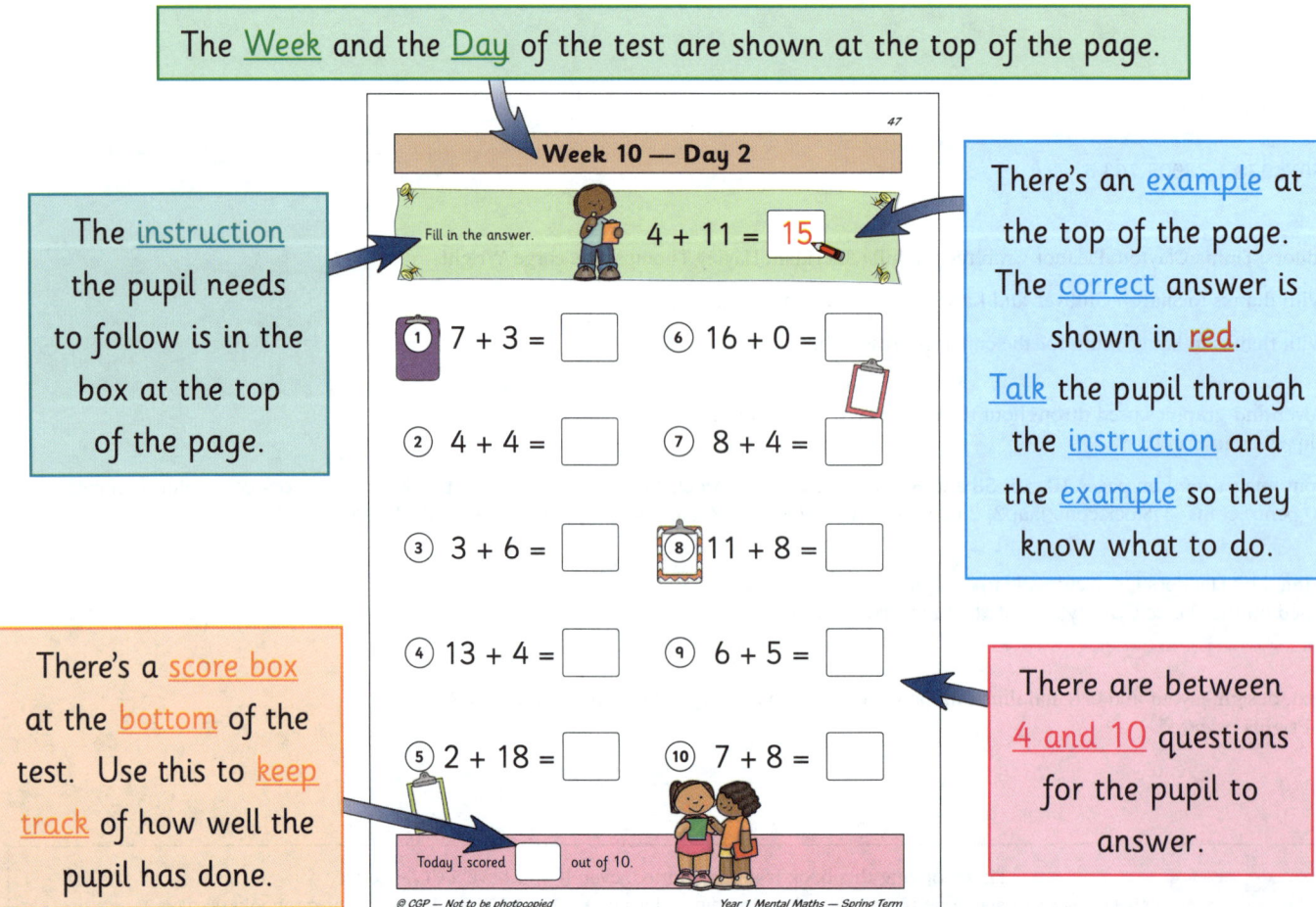

Week 1 — Day 1

Counting upwards, what are the next two numbers after the number shown?

22 | 23 | 24

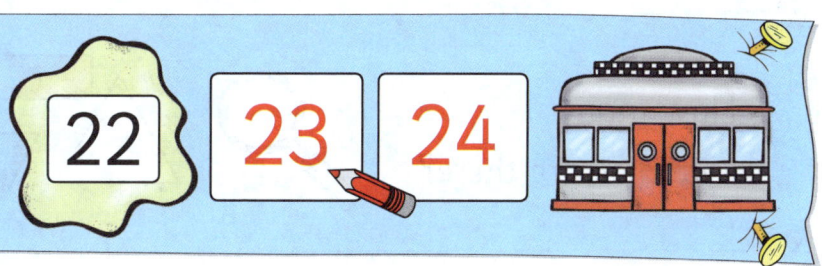

1. 5 | ☐ | ☐

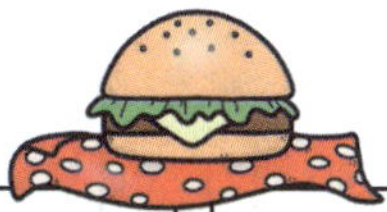

2. 12 | ☐ | ☐

3. 34 | ☐ | ☐

4. 21 | ☐ | ☐

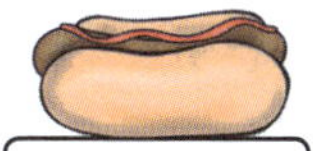

5. 26 | ☐ | ☐

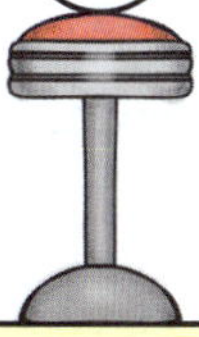

6. 42 | ☐ | ☐

7. 37 | ☐ | ☐

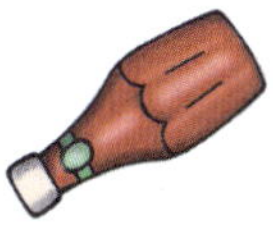

8. 28 | ☐ | ☐

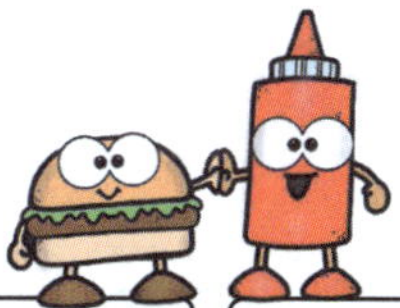

9. 44 | ☐ | ☐

10. 39 | ☐ | ☐

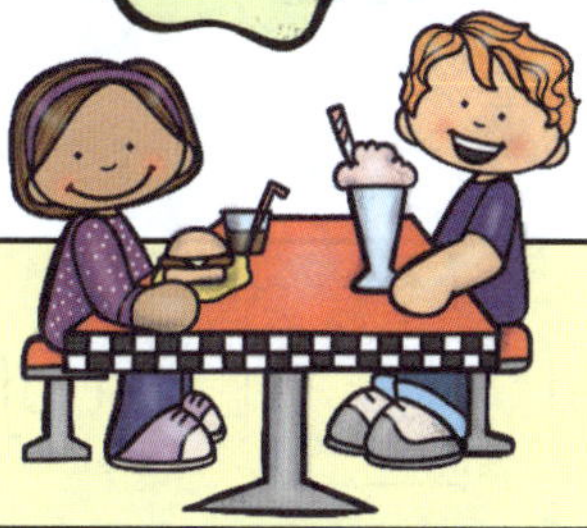

Today I scored ☐ out of 10.

Week 1 — Day 3

Work out the answer.   14 − 5 = 9

1) 4 − 1 =

2) 7 − 2 =

3) 6 − 4 =

4) 9 − 6 =

5) 10 − 8 =

6) 14 − 0 =

7) 12 − 3 =

8) 19 − 5 =

9) 14 − 7 =

10) 16 − 7 =

Today I scored [ ] out of 10.

Week 1 — Day 4

Complete the sentence. Use the pictures to help you.  Half of 4 is [2]

1)  Half of 2 is ☐

2)  Double 4 is ☐

3)  Double 10 is ☐

4)  Half of 6 is ☐

5)  Half of 12 is ☐

6)  Double 8 is ☐

7) Half of 18 is ☐

Today I scored ☐ out of 7.

Year 1 Mental Maths — Spring Term © CGP — Not to be photocopied

Week 1 — Day 5

Circle the child with fewer fish. Then write the number of fish that the children have altogether.

Tim: I have 3 fish.
Rui: I have 7 fish.
Altogether: 10

1) Cathy: I have 3 fish. Matt: I have 4 fish. Altogether: ☐

2) Miko: I have 10 fish. Sophie: I have 7 fish. Altogether: ☐

3) Sadie: I have 8 fish. Toby: I have 4 fish. Altogether: ☐

4) Jorge: I have 4 fish. Oscar: I have 15 fish. Altogether: ☐

Today I scored ☐ out of 4.

Week 2 — Day 1

Count in steps of two to fill in the missing numbers

16   **18**   20   **22**

1) 10   ☐   14   ☐   18

2) 22   24   ☐   28   ☐

3) 8   ☐   12   14   ☐

4) 16   18   ☐   ☐   24

5) 36   ☐   ☐   42   44

Today I scored ☐ out of 5.

Year 1 Mental Maths — Spring Term

Week 2 — Day 2

Write the bigger number in words.   15 18   eighteen

1) 3 9

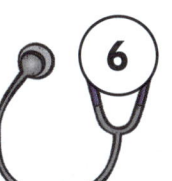

6) 17 8

2) 15 4

7) 10 13

3) 8 7

8) 11 9

4) 12 10

9) 20 12

5) 16 14

10) 18 19

Today I scored ☐ out of 10.

Week 2 — Day 3

Fill in the answer. 7 add 3 = 10

1) 5 add 2 =

6) 13 add 4 =

2) 3 add 3 =

7) 4 add 7 =

3) 1 add 4 =

8) 9 add 3 =

4) 6 add 2 =

9) 2 add 18 =

5) 5 add 10 =

10) 6 add 12 =

Today I scored ☐ out of 10.

Week 2 — Day 4

Circle the two numbers that you say when counting from 10 to 30. 45 (24) 6 (13)

1) 50 15 20 3 6 9 11 19 32

2) 12 28 44 39

7) 36 42 26 23

3) 35 16 4 22

8) 1 21 38 16

4) 17 37 7 27

9) 25 34 14 43

5) 18 29 2 41

10) 31 19 29 49

Today I scored ☐ out of 10.

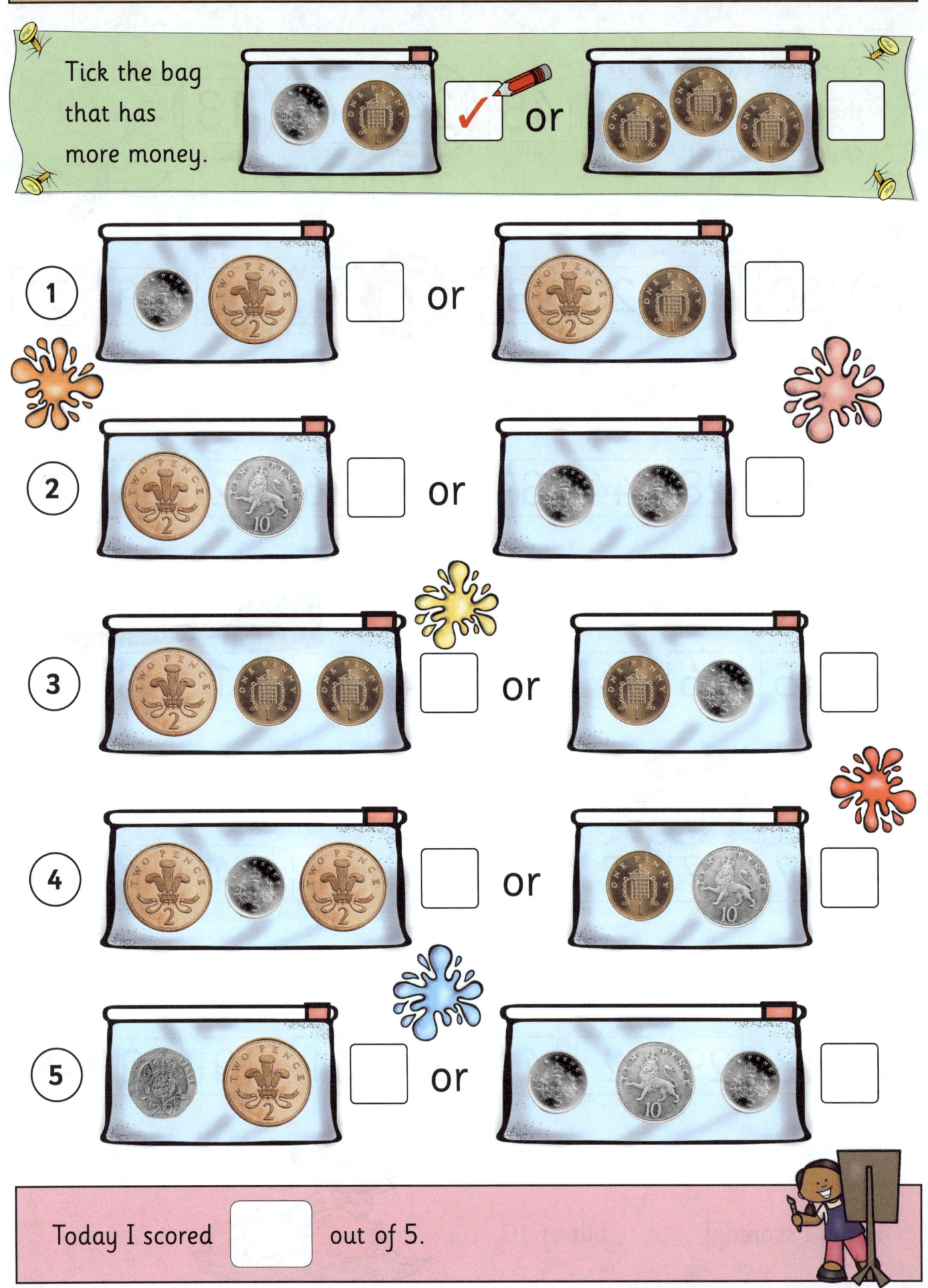

Week 3 — Day 1

Put the numbers in order from biggest to smallest. Then write the next number in the pattern in the pink box.

17	19	16	18
19	18	17	16	15

1) 11 14 12 13

2) 27 24 25 26

3) 10 7 8 9

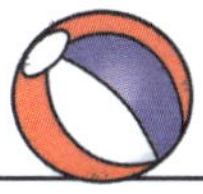

4) 44 42 45 43

5) 32 33 30 31

6) 50 48 49 51

Today I scored ☐ out of 6.

Week 3 — Day 2

Count the marbles.
Are there more or fewer than the number shown?
Circle your answer.

1)  more   fewer

2)  more   fewer

3)  more   fewer

4)  more   fewer

5)  more   fewer

6)  more   fewer

7)  more   fewer

8)  more   fewer

Today I scored ☐ out of 8.

Week 3 — Day 3

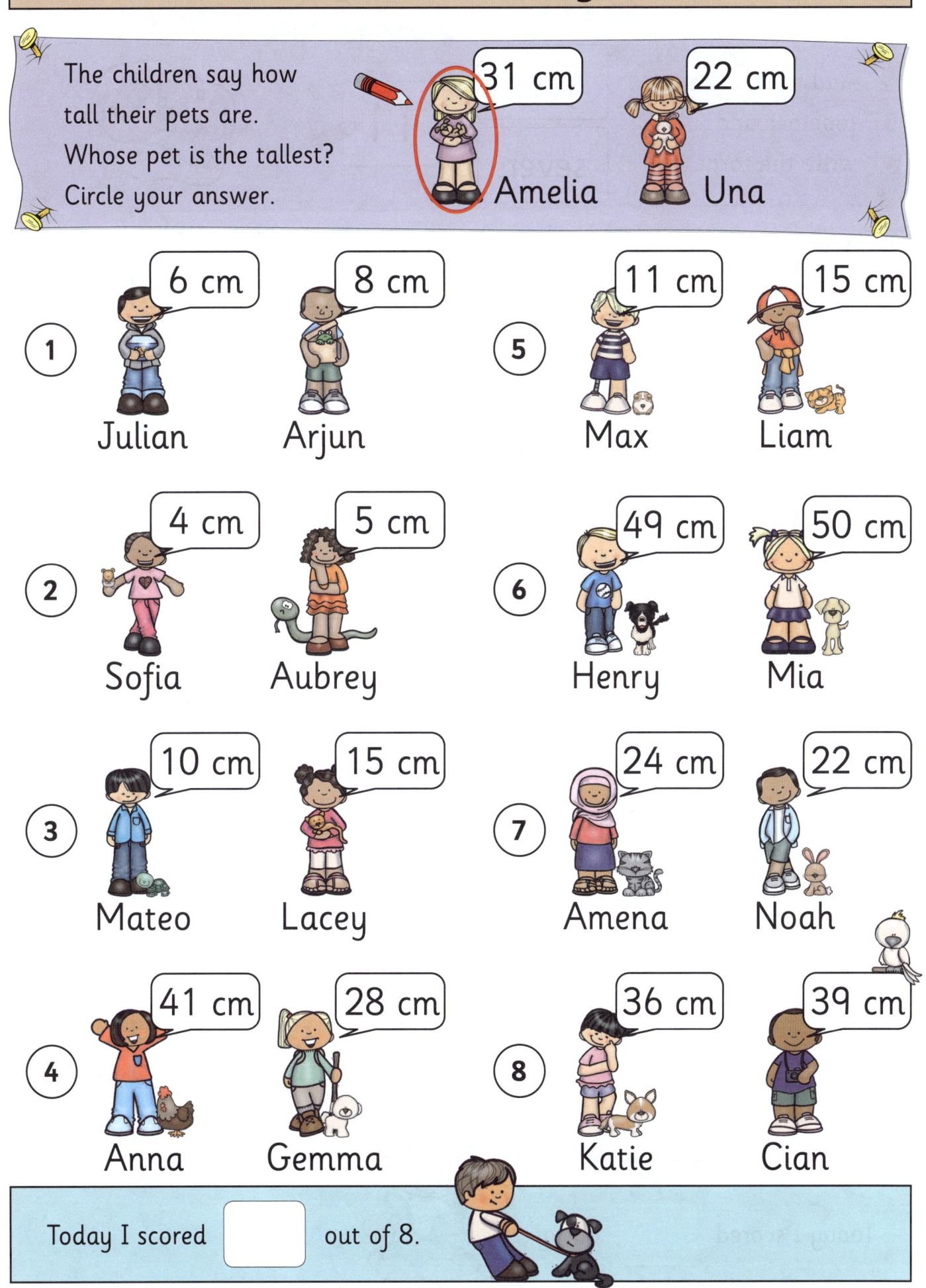

The children say how tall their pets are.
Whose pet is the tallest?
Circle your answer.

Amelia 31 cm, Una 22 cm

1. Julian 6 cm, Arjun 8 cm
2. Sofia 4 cm, Aubrey 5 cm
3. Mateo 10 cm, Lacey 15 cm
4. Anna 41 cm, Gemma 28 cm
5. Max 11 cm, Liam 15 cm
6. Henry 49 cm, Mia 50 cm
7. Amena 24 cm, Noah 22 cm
8. Katie 36 cm, Cian 39 cm

Today I scored ☐ out of 8.

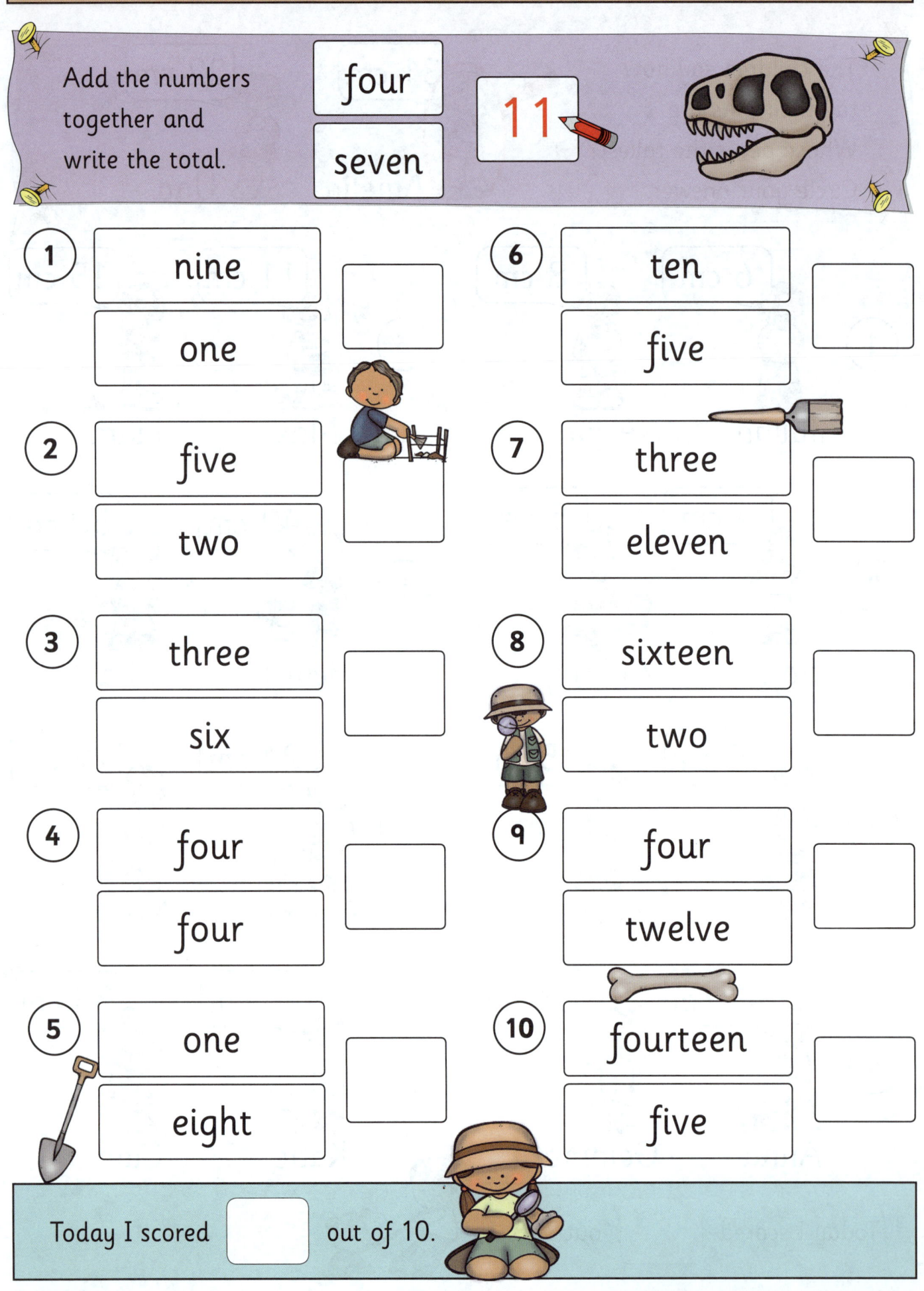

Week 3 — Day 5

Take away 3 flowers. How many are left?

Example: 7 flowers − 3 = **4**

1. (4 flowers) ☐

2. (6 flowers) ☐

3. (9 flowers) ☐

4. (8 flowers) ☐

5. (13 flowers) ☐

6. (10 flowers) ☐

7. (14 flowers) ☐

8. (16 flowers) ☐

Today I scored ☐ out of 8.

Week 4 — Day 1

Circle the number that is one more than the number shown.

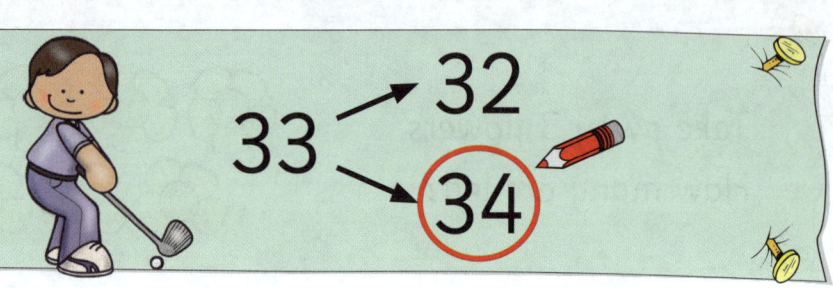
33 → 32
33 → (34)

1) 7 → 8 / 5
2) 3 → 4 / 2
3) 9 → 10 / 8
4) 15 → 20 / 16
5) 26 → 24 / 27

6) 44 → 45 / 46
7) 11 → 10 / 12
8) 19 → 20 / 21
9) 37 → 36 / 38
10) 49 → 40 / 50

Today I scored ☐ out of 10.

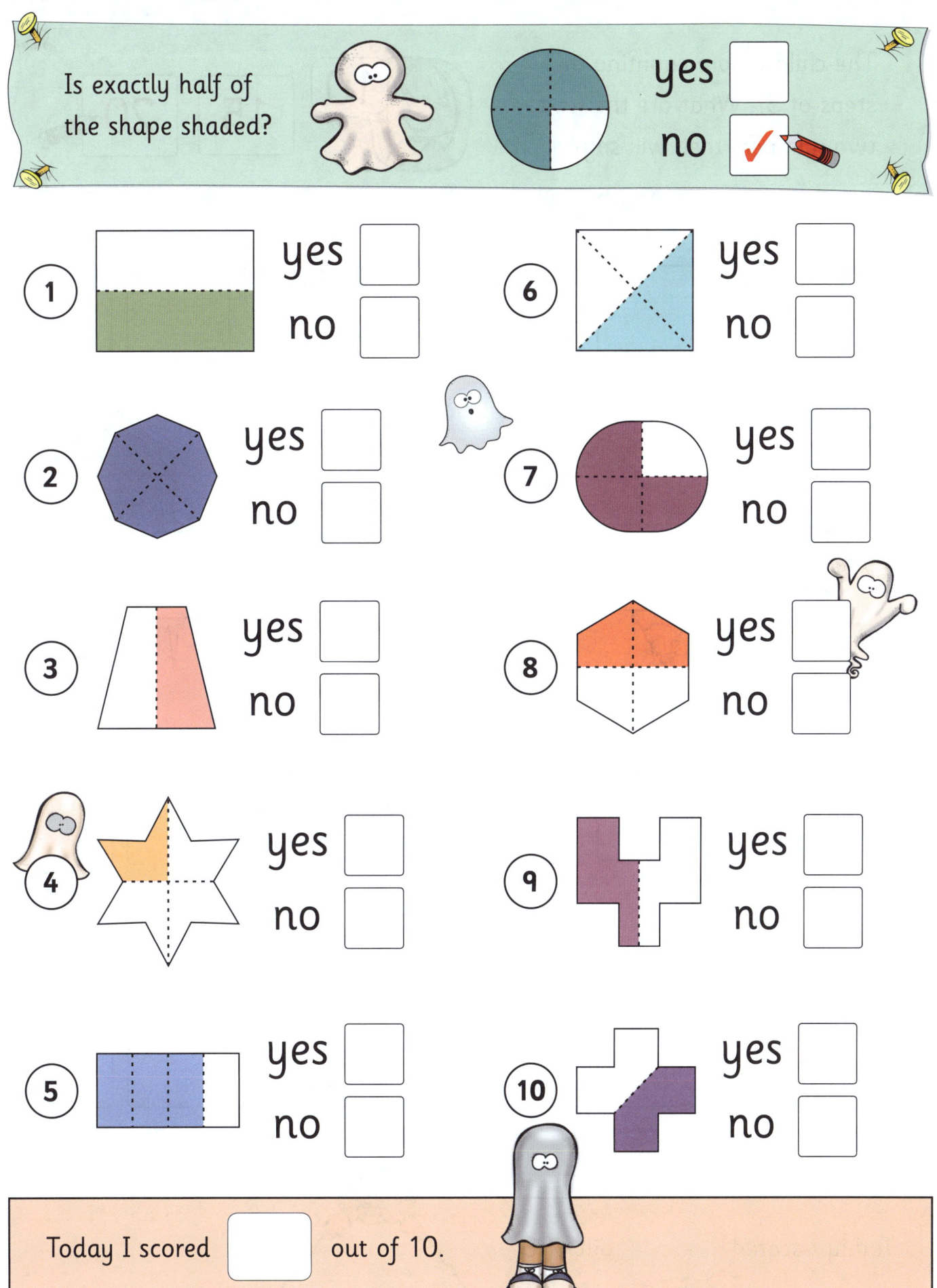

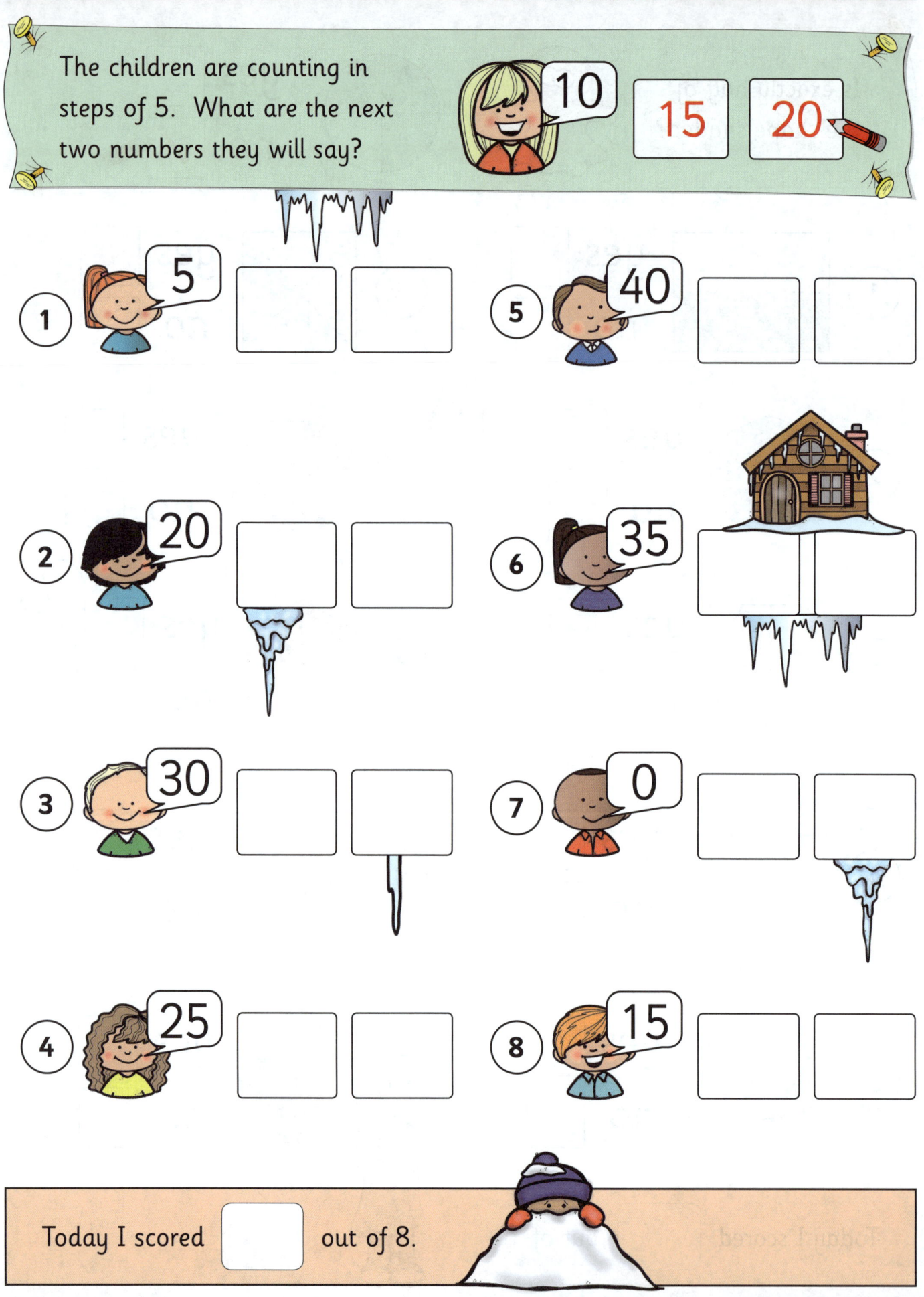

Week 4 — Day 4

Circle the calculation that equals 10.

(5 + 5) ⬅ circled

16 − 3

1. 9 + 1
    9 − 1

2. 12 − 2
    8 − 2

3. 7 − 4
    7 + 3

4. 16 + 4
    11 − 1

5. 10 + 1
    15 − 5

6. 8 + 2
    9 + 2

7. 19 − 9
    16 − 4

8. 10 − 1
    13 − 3

9. 6 + 4
    9 − 5

10. 3 + 9
    18 − 8

Today I scored ☐ out of 10.

Week 4 — Day 5

Jack counts in steps of 10 from 0. Circle the numbers that Jack says.
June counts in steps of 5 from 0. Put a cross through the numbers that June says.

43   ⊗20   ⊗35   4

1) 5   29   12   37   30

2) 2   15   10   33   48

3) 41   40   16   29   25

4) 50   45   1   19   21

Today I scored ☐ out of 4.

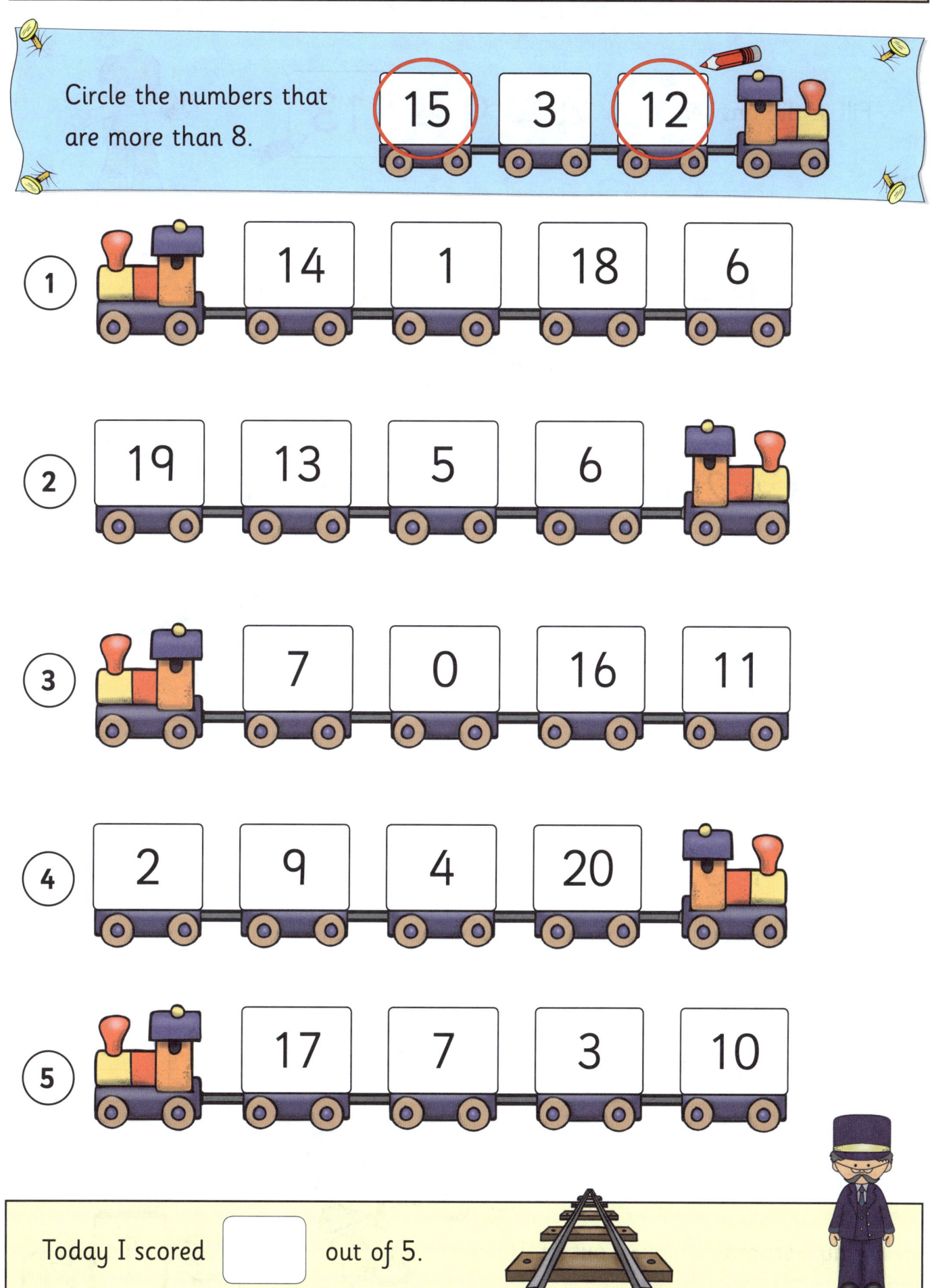

Week 5 — Day 2

Fill in the answer.   4 + 9 = 13

1) 1 + 8 =

2) 13 + 2 =

3) 7 + 0 =

4) 14 + 0 =

5) 5 + 10 =

6) 0 + 8 =

7) 11 + 6 =

8) 7 + 7 =

9) 0 + 0 =

10) 5 + 15 =

Today I scored ☐ out of 10.

Week 5 — Day 3

Subtract the smallest number from the largest number.

5 6 9 2

9 − 2 = 7

1) 1 3 2 4

☐ − ☐ = ☐

5) 18 10 1 20

☐ − ☐ = ☐

2) 7 10 3 6

☐ − ☐ = ☐

6) 15 5 4 14

☐ − ☐ = ☐

3) 8 5 4 6

☐ − ☐ = ☐

7) 13 5 9 17

☐ − ☐ = ☐

4) 12 10 2 0

☐ − ☐ = ☐

8) 5 12 14 8

☐ − ☐ = ☐

Today I scored ☐ out of 8.

Week 5 — Day 4

How many more apples does the giraffe need to have the same number as the elephant?

1.

5.

2.

6.

3.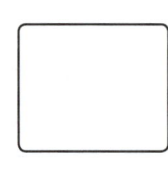

7.

4.

8.

Today I scored 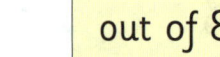 out of 8.

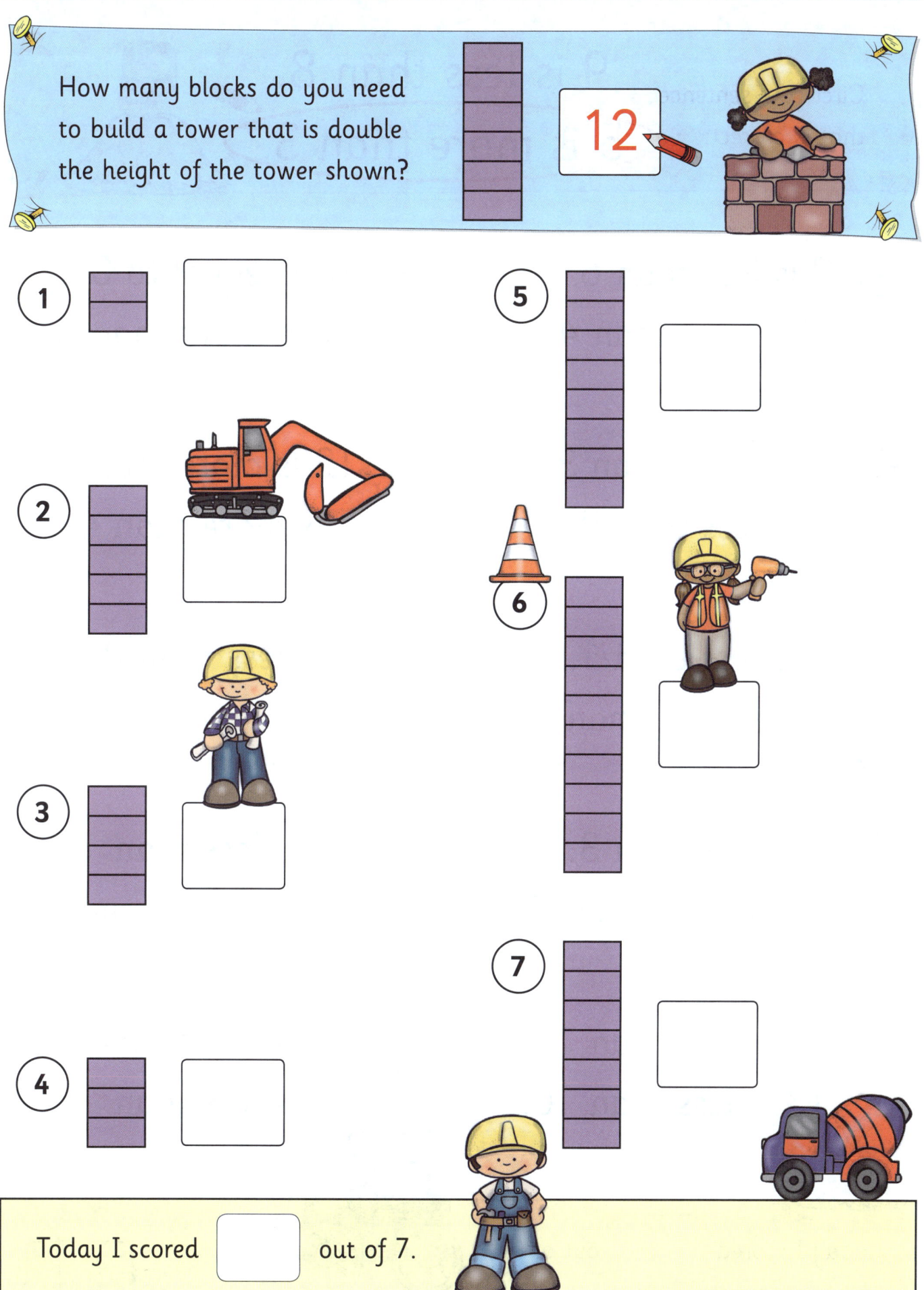

Week 6 — Day 1

Circle the sentence that is correct.

9 is less than 8.
~~(5 is more than 3.)~~

1. 2 is less than 6.
10 is less than 4.

2. 1 is more than 3.
7 is less than 9.

3. 5 is less than 1.
16 is more than 6.

4. 8 is less than 3.
15 is more than 7.

5. 11 is less than 19.
13 is less than 10.

6. 10 is equal to 0.
12 is more than 8.

7. 12 is more than 14.
5 is more than 4.

8. 6 is less than 8.
16 is more than 17.

9. 11 is less than 13.
13 is more than 16.

10. 18 is more than 19.
17 is less than 18.

Today I scored ☐ out of 10.

Week 6 — Day 2

Count backwards to fill in the missing numbers.

| 14 | 13 | 12 | 11 | 10 |

1) | 18 | 17 | 16 | | |

2) | 35 | 34 | 33 | | |

3) | 22 | 21 | 20 | | |

4) | 50 | 49 | 48 | | |

5) | 43 | 42 | 41 | | |

Today I scored ☐ out of 5.

Week 6 — Day 3

Circle the correct calculation.

$4 + 2 = 6$ (circled)
$4 - 2 = 6$

1. $2 + 1 = 3$
   $2 - 1 = 3$

2. $10 + 2 = 8$
   $10 - 2 = 8$

3. $7 + 3 = 10$
   $7 - 3 = 10$

4. $9 + 2 = 11$
   $9 - 2 = 11$

5. $14 + 4 = 18$
   $14 - 4 = 18$

6. $15 + 5 = 10$
   $15 - 5 = 10$

7. $8 + 6 = 14$
   $8 - 6 = 14$

8. $7 + 4 = 3$
   $7 - 4 = 3$

9. $11 + 4 = 15$
   $11 - 4 = 15$

10. $18 + 2 = 16$
    $18 - 2 = 16$

Today I scored ☐ out of 10.

Week 6 — Day 4

Count in steps of 5 to find the missing numbers.

10 **15** 20 **25**

1) 5 ☐ 15 ☐ 25

2) 20 25 ☐ 35 ☐

3) 15 ☐ ☐ 30 35

4) 0 ☐ 10 ☐ 20

5) ☐ 30 ☐ 40 45

Today I scored ☐ out of 5.

Week 6 — Day 5

Circle the two numbers that add up to make the number on the blackboard.

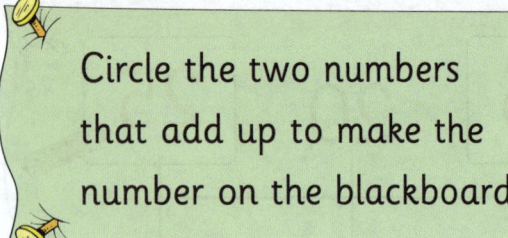  5 | 3 | ① | 8 | ④

1.  7 — 9 | 2 | 10 | 5 | 1

2.  10 — 5 | 12 | 1 | 7 | 3

3.  9 — 4 | 3 | 11 | 5 | 7

4.  15 — 10 | 3 | 12 | 1 | 17

5.  8 — 3 | 4 | 1 | 6 | 5

Today I scored ☐ out of 5.

Week 7 — Day 1

Write the numbers that are one more and one less than the number shown.

one less		one more
24	25	26

1. one less ☐ 17 one more ☐

2. one less ☐ 23 one more ☐

3. one less ☐ 11 one more ☐

4. one less ☐ 39 one more ☐

5. one less ☐ 46 one more ☐

6. one less ☐ 52 one more ☐

7. one less ☐ 68 one more ☐

8. one less ☐ 40 one more ☐

9. one less ☐ 75 one more ☐

10. one less ☐ 70 one more ☐

Today I scored ☐ out of 10.

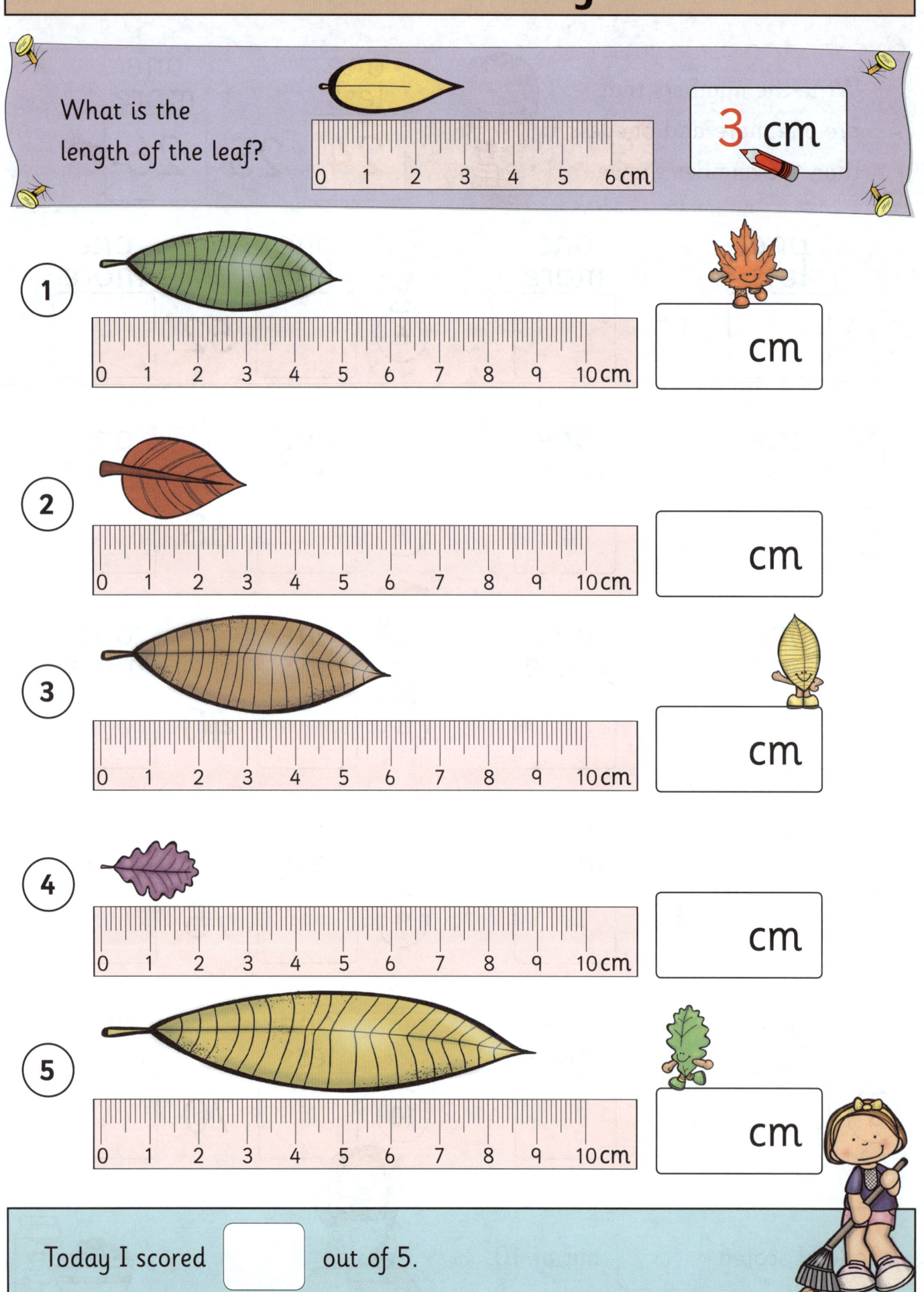

Week 7 — Day 3

The number of cows on a farm is two more than the number on the sheep. How many cows are there?

   1

   6

   2

   7

   3

   8

   4

   9

   5

   10

Today I scored ☐ out of 10.

Week 7 — Day 4

The number of flies each frog has eaten is shown. How many flies did they eat in total? Complete the number sentence.

1

5

2

6

3

7

4

8

Today I scored ☐ out of 8.

Week 7 — Day 5

Find the difference between the two numbers. 13 2 11

1) 6 2 ☐

6) 17 7 ☐

2) 5 3 ☐

7) 20 3 ☐

3) 7 4 ☐

8) 12 5 ☐

4) 10 3 ☐

9) 16 8 ☐

5) 15 6 ☐

10) 13 8 ☐

Today I scored ☐ out of 10.

Week 8 — Day 1

Write + or – to match the word. Then write the answer.

6 add 4 = | 6 | + | 4 | = | 10 |

1) 15 subtract 7 = | 15 | | 7 | = | |

2) 0 add 11 = | 0 | | 11 | = | |

3) 12 subtract 8 = | 12 | | 8 | = | |

4) 17 subtract 0 = | 17 | | 0 | = | |

5) 6 add 13 = | 6 | | 13 | = | |

Today I scored ☐ out of 5.

Week 8 — Day 2

A carrot weighs 30 grams. Write down the weight of the food shown. Is it heavier or lighter than the carrot?

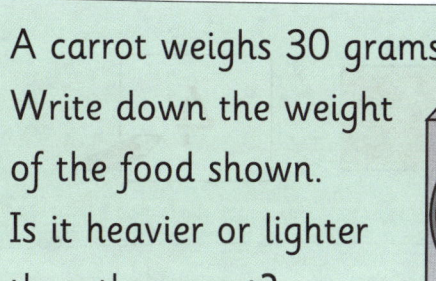

10 grams

The tomato is heavier / ~~lighter~~ than the 30 gram carrot.

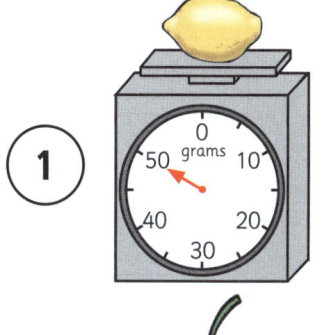

1) _____ grams

The lemon is heavier / lighter than the 30 gram carrot.

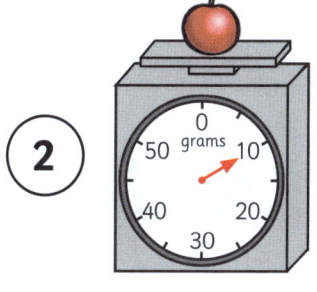

2) _____ grams

The cherry is heavier / lighter than the 30 gram carrot.

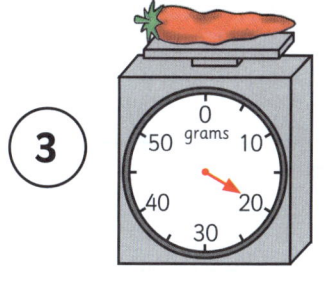

3) _____ grams

The chilli is heavier / lighter than the 30 gram carrot.

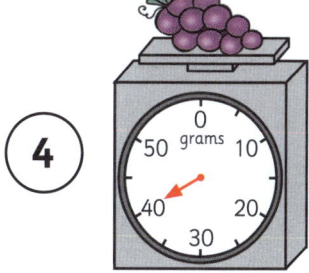

4) _____ grams

The grapes are heavier / lighter than the 30 gram carrot.

Today I scored _____ out of 4.

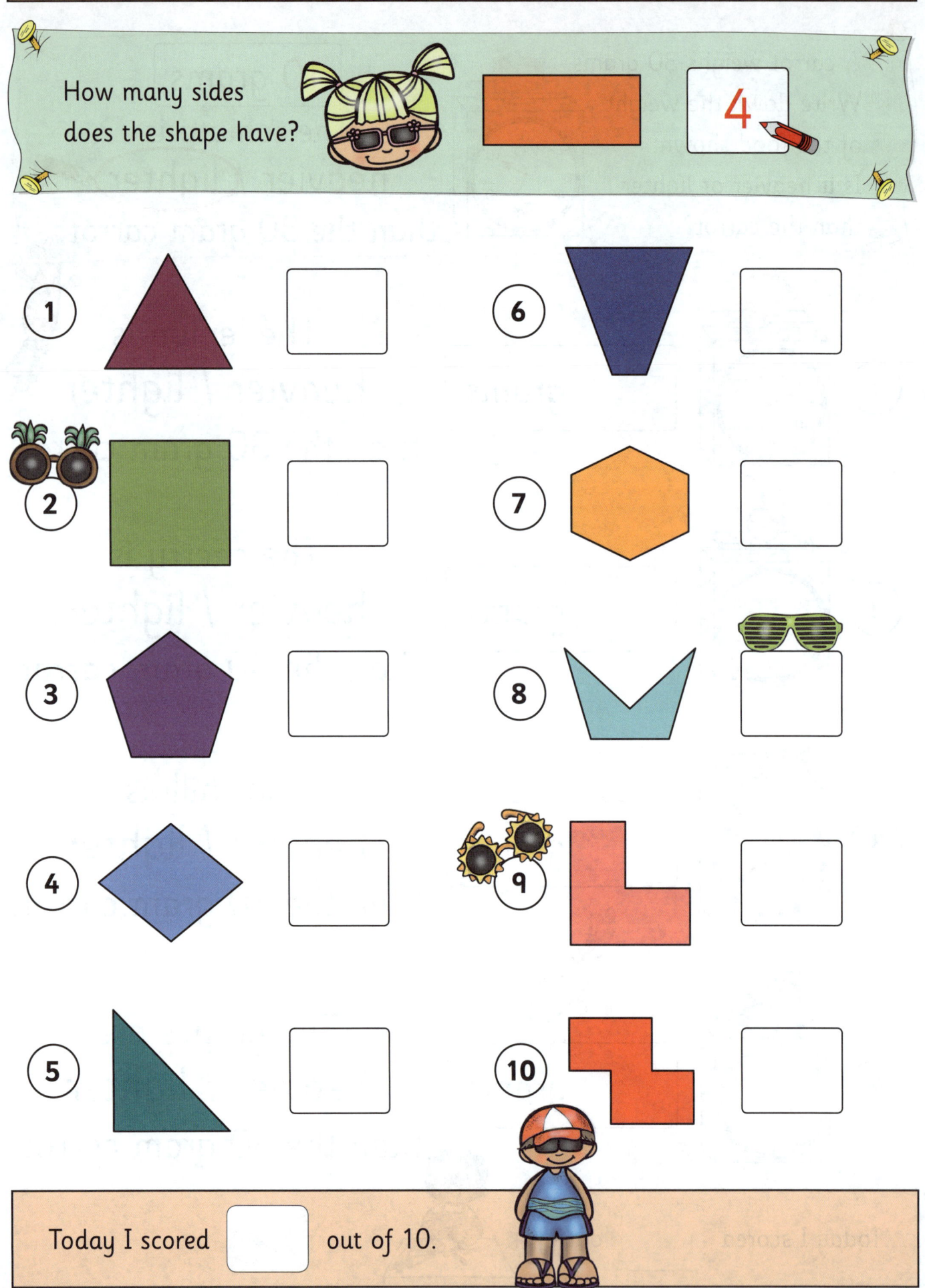

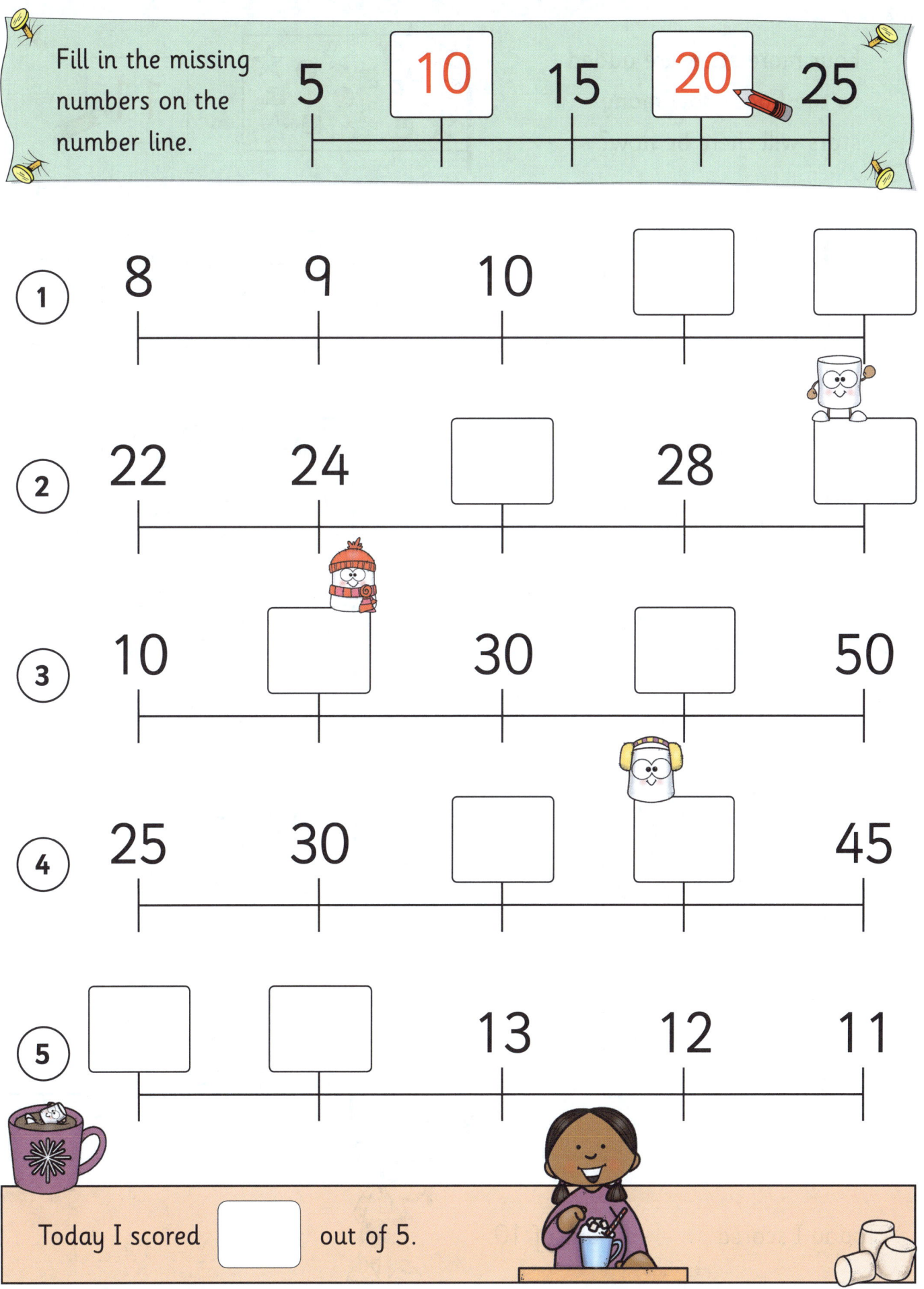

Week 8 — Day 5

Four more stars are added to the flag. How many stars will there be now?

1.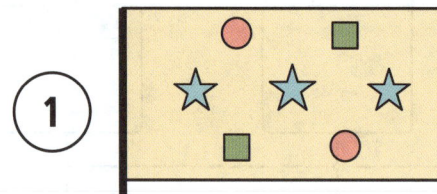
2.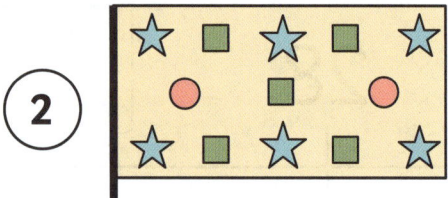
3.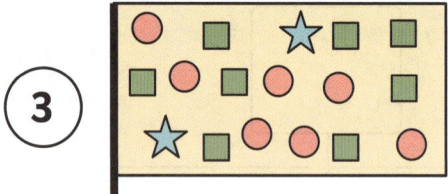
4.
5.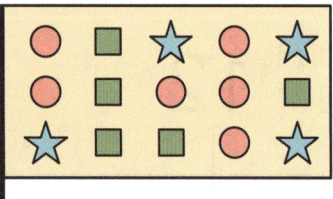
6.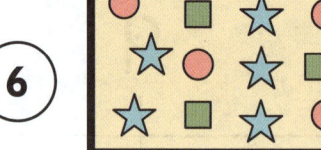
7.
8.
9.
10.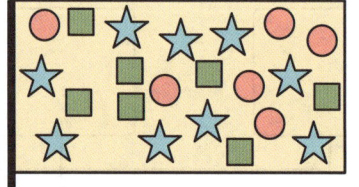

Today I scored ☐ out of 10.

Week 9 — Day 1

Leon starts from 0 and counts upwards in steps of 5. Cross out any numbers he won't say.

~~8~~   35   20   ~~11~~

1) 5   34   30   19

2) 44   50   15   20

3) 17   25   24   40

4) 45   10   8   49

5) 6   19   50   26

6) 16   54   22   15

7) 4   35   21   45

8) 25   10   28   30

9) 14   18   24   20

10) 43   40   15   39

Today I scored ☐ out of 10.

Week 9 — Day 2

A baker has 16 doughnuts.
He sells the number shown.
How many are left?

He sells 4. 12

1) He sells 5.

2) He sells 10.

3) He sells 6.

4) He sells 0.

5) He sells 8.

6) He sells 9.

7) He sells 15.

8) He sells 16.

9) He sells 13.

10) He sells 11.

Today I scored ☐ out of 10.

Week 9 — Day 3

Do the two numbers add up to 20?

fifteen three ☐ yes ✓ no

1. eighteen two ☐ yes ☐ no

2.  nine five ☐ yes ☐ no

3. ten ten ☐ yes ☐ no

4. five fifteen ☐ yes ☐ no

5.  eleven nine ☐ yes ☐ no

6. nine eight ☐ yes ☐ no

7. six twelve ☐ yes ☐ no

8.  twenty zero ☐ yes ☐ no

9. seven thirteen ☐ yes ☐ no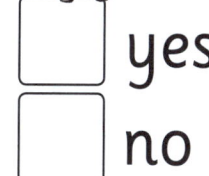

10. thirteen six ☐ yes ☐ no

Today I scored ☐ out of 10.

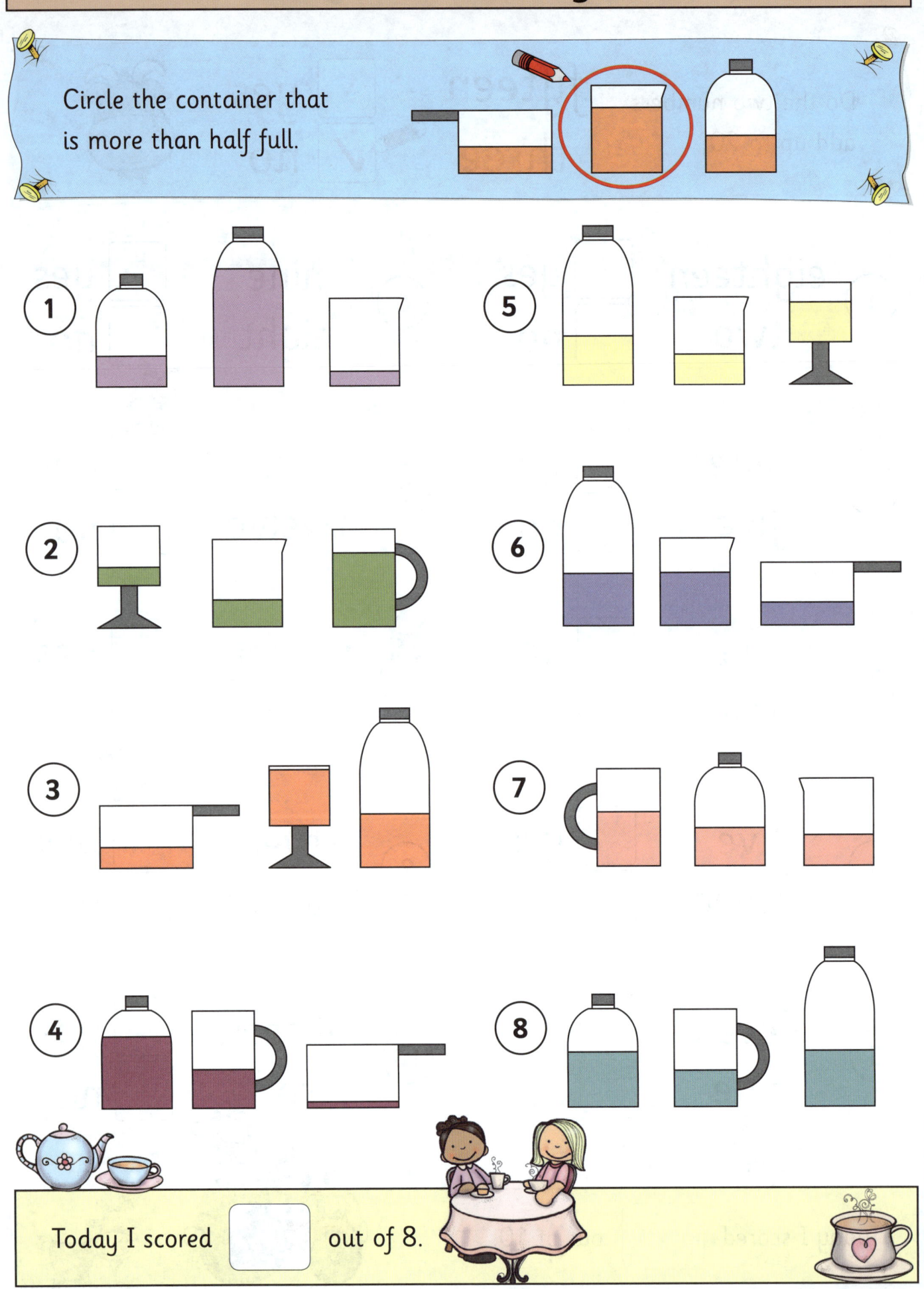

Week 9 — Day 5

Work out the total amount of money.   2p + 10p = **12p**

1. 1p + 2p = ___ p

2. 10p + 1p = ___ p

3. 1p + 2p = ___ p

4. 1p + 1p + 2p = ___ p

5. 1p + 1p + 1p = ___ p

6. 10p + 10p + 10p = ___ p

7. 1p + 10p + 1p = ___ p

8. 20p + 1p + 2p = ___ p

Today I scored ☐ out of 8.

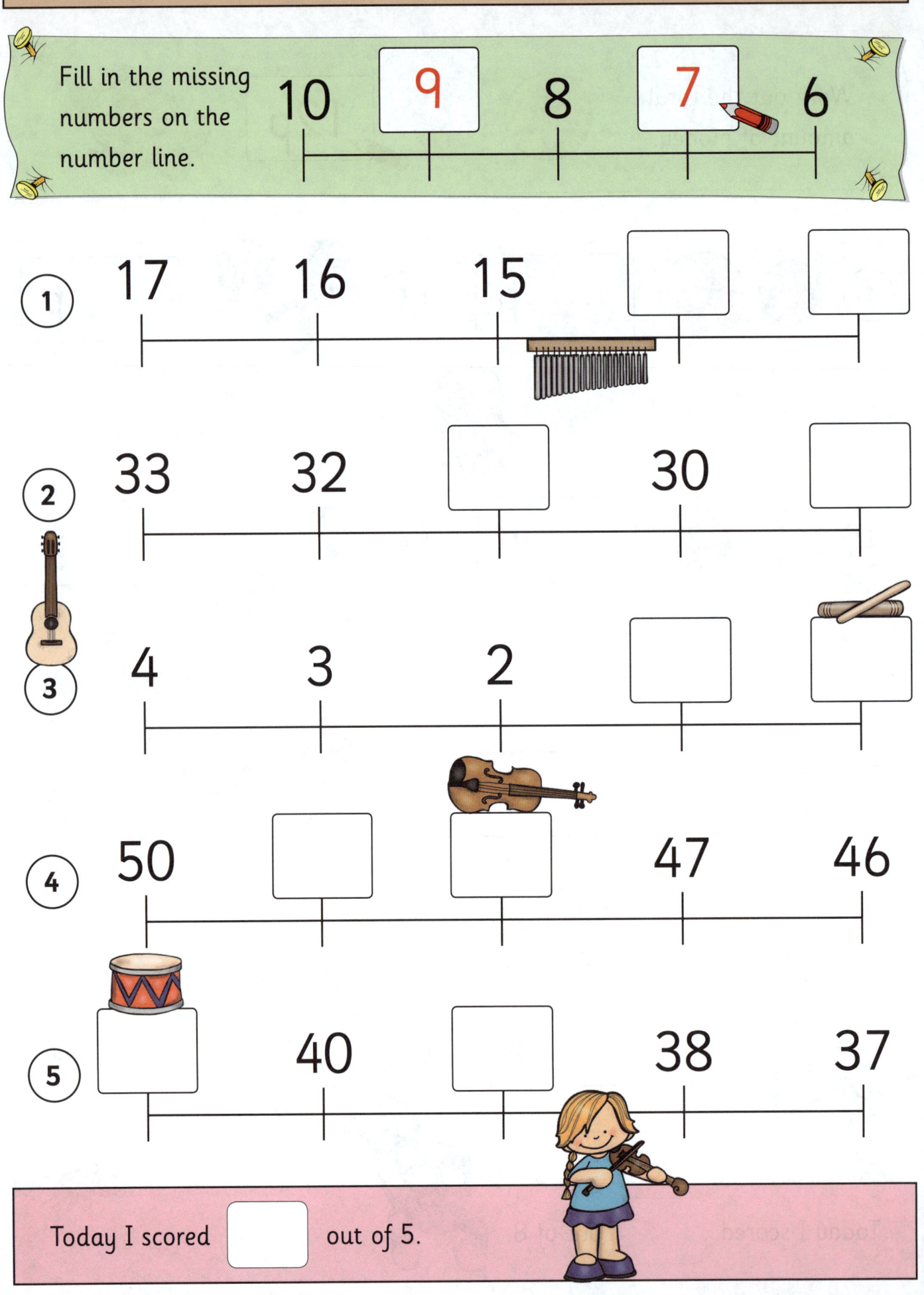

Week 10 — Day 2

Fill in the answer.  4 + 11 = 15

 7 + 3 = ☐   ⑥ 16 + 0 = ☐

② 4 + 4 = ☐   ⑦ 8 + 4 = ☐

③ 3 + 6 = ☐    11 + 8 = ☐

④ 13 + 4 = ☐   ⑨ 6 + 5 = ☐

 2 + 18 = ☐   ⑩ 7 + 8 = ☐

Today I scored ☐ out of 10.

Week 10 — Day 3

Circle any jug with 4 or more litres of liquid in it.

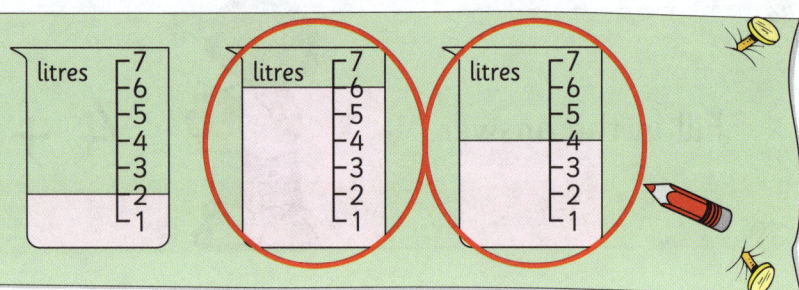

1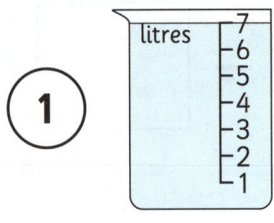

2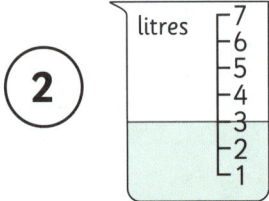

3

4

5

Today I scored ☐ out of 5.

Week 10 — Day 4

Write the number that is being described.

1 more than 13. 14

1. 1 less than 36.
2. 2 more than 22.
3. 5 less than 20.
4. 1 more than 59.
5. 3 less than 12.
6. 10 more than 9.
7. 10 less than 11.
8. 14 more than 3.
9. 7 less than 18.
10. 9 more than 8.

Today I scored ☐ out of 10.

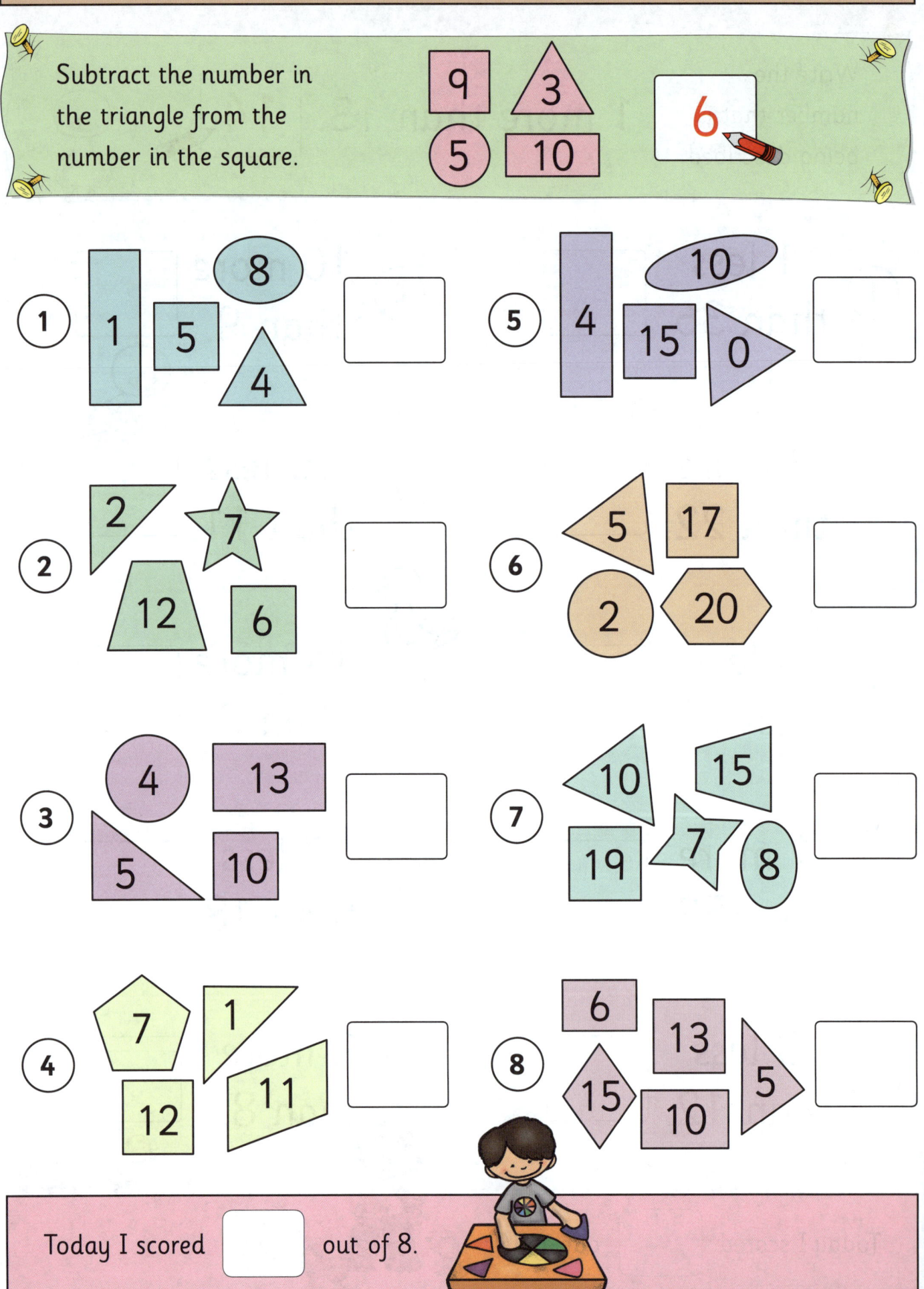

Week 11 — Day 1

Write the answer in words.

One add eight is **nine**

1) Two add four is

2) Four add five is

3) Ten add seven is

4) Six add four is

5) Eleven add two is

6) Five add six is

7) Twelve add two is

8) Fifteen add three is

9) Nine add three is

10) Sixteen add zero is

Today I scored ☐ out of 10.

Week 11 — Day 2

Tick the box if the answer to the subtraction is right. Cross the box if the answer is wrong.

20 − 1 = 11 ✗
20 − 5 = 15 ✓

1) 20 − 2 = 16 ☐

2) 20 − 15 = 5 ☐

3) 20 − 4 = 16 ☐

4) 20 − 7 = 11 ☐

5) 20 − 11 = 8 ☐

6) 20 − 6 = 14 ☐

7) 20 − 18 = 3 ☐

8) 20 − 13 = 7 ☐

9) 20 − 9 = 10 ☐

10) 20 − 8 = 12 ☐

Today I scored ☐ out of 10.

Week 11 — Day 3

The number of items on the washing line is shown. 4 items blow away. How many are left?

1.

2.

3.

4.

5. 16

6. 7

7. 9

8.

9. 17

10. 11

Today I scored ☐ out of 10.

Week 11 — Day 4

Complete the sentence. Use the pictures to help you.

Half of 2 is 1

① Half of 4 is ☐

④ Half of 10 is ☐

② Half of 6 is ☐

⑤ Half of 12 is ☐

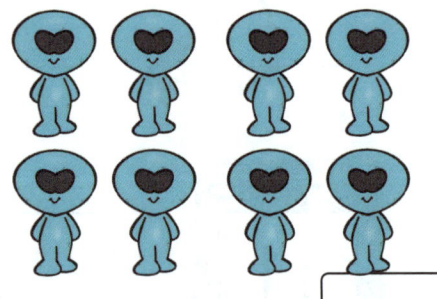

③ Half of 8 is ☐

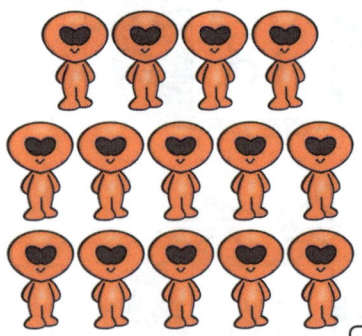

⑥ Half of 14 is ☐

Today I scored ☐ out of 6.

Week 11 — Day 5

Chloe ate 12 frogs. How many did the other crocodiles eat?

Mo ate 1 more frog than Chloe. **13**

1) Charlie ate 1 less frog than Chloe.

2) Benula ate 2 more frogs than Chloe.

3) Siobhan ate 4 fewer frogs than Chloe.

4) Bea ate 8 more frogs than Chloe.

5) Zac ate 6 fewer frogs than Chloe.

6) Matteo ate 7 more frogs than Chloe.

Today I scored ☐ out of 6.

Week 12 — Day 1

Tick the box if the amount of money is the same as it says on the sign. Cross the box if not.

1  

5

2

6

3

7

4

8

Today I scored out of 8.

Week 12 — Day 2

Circle any numbers you say when counting in twos from the pink number to the blue number.

12 → 22
10 (14) 17 (20)

1. 0 → 10
   1 3 6 9

2. 10 → 20
   13 14 17 18

3. 30 → 40
   32 35 38 44

4. 20 → 30
   21 22 29 34

5. 4 → 14
   2 8 11 12

6. 16 → 26
   18 20 24 30

7. 22 → 32
   25 26 31 35

8. 34 → 44
   26 36 40 43

9. 28 → 38
   30 31 33 36

10. 40 → 50
    36 42 48 49

Today I scored ☐ out of 10.

Week 12 — Day 3

Fill in the box so that the two numbers add up to the number in the hexagon.

3 + [5] = 8

1) 6 + ☐ = 10

2) ☐ + 4 = 12

3) 7 + ☐ = 14

4) 5 + ☐ = 9

5) ☐ + 8 = 11

6) 9 + ☐ = 16

7) ☐ + 7 = 13

8) 5 + ☐ = 18

9) ☐ + 17 = 20

10) 8 + ☐ = 15

Today I scored ☐ out of 10.

Week 12 — Day 4

Farrah pours 4 more litres of lemonade into the jug. How much lemonade is in the jug now?

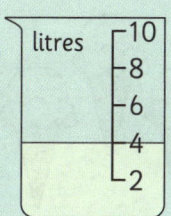 

1 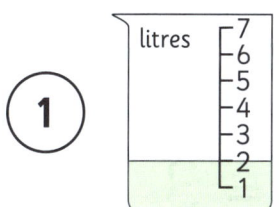 ☐ litres

2  ☐ litres

3 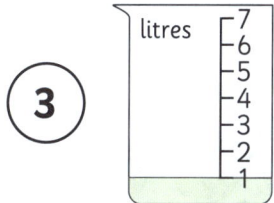 ☐ litres

4 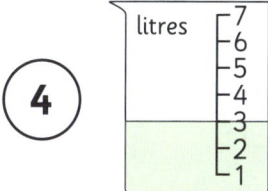 ☐ litres

5 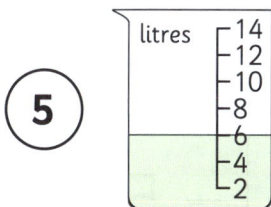  ☐ litres

6   ☐ litres

7 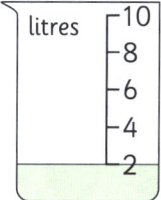 ☐ litres

8  ☐ litres

9  ☐ litres

10  ☐ litres

Today I scored ☐ out of 10.

Week 12 — Day 5

What is the missing number? Use the pictures to help you.

$4 - \boxed{3} = 1$

①

$5 - \boxed{} = 3$

⑤

$7 - \boxed{} = 3$

②

$10 - \boxed{} = 3$

⑥

$9 - \boxed{} = 4$

③

$8 - \boxed{} = 5$

⑦

$11 - \boxed{} = 3$

④

$14 - \boxed{} = 8$

⑧

$12 - \boxed{} = 5$

Today I scored 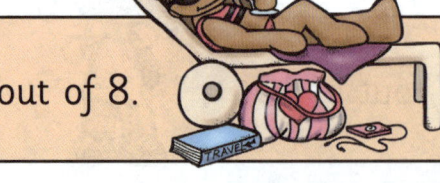 out of 8.

Answers

Week 1 — Day 1
1. 6, 7
2. 13, 14
3. 35, 36
4. 22, 23
5. 27, 28
6. 43, 44
7. 38, 39
8. 29, 30
9. 45, 46
10. 40, 41

Week 1 — Day 2
1. 2
2. 1
3. 2
4. 3
5. 1
6. 2
7. 2
8. 3
9. 4
10. 3

Week 1 — Day 3
1. 3
2. 5
3. 2
4. 3
5. 2
6. 14
7. 9
8. 14
9. 7
10. 9

Week 1 — Day 4
1. 1
2. 8
3. 20
4. 3
5. 6
6. 16
7. 9

Week 1 — Day 5
1. Cathy, 7
2. Sophie, 17
3. Toby, 12
4. Jorge, 19

Week 2 — Day 1
1. 12, 16
2. 26, 30
3. 10, 16
4. 20, 22
5. 38, 40

Week 2 — Day 2
1. nine
2. fifteen
3. eight
4. twelve
5. sixteen
6. seventeen
7. thirteen
8. eleven
9. twenty
10. nineteen

Week 2 — Day 3
1. 7
2. 6
3. 5
4. 8
5. 15
6. 17
7. 11
8. 12
9. 20
10. 18

Week 2 — Day 4
1. 15, 20
2. 12, 28
3. 16, 22
4. 17, 27
5. 18, 29
6. 11, 19
7. 26, 23
8. 21, 16
9. 25, 14
10. 19, 29

Week 2 — Day 5
1.
2.
3.
4.
5.

Week 3 — Day 1
1. 14, 13, 12, 11, 10
2. 27, 26, 25, 24, 23
3. 10, 9, 8, 7, 6
4. 45, 44, 43, 42, 41
5. 33, 32, 31, 30, 29
6. 51, 50, 49, 48, 47

Week 3 — Day 2
1. fewer
2. fewer
3. more
4. more
5. more
6. fewer
7. more
8. fewer

Week 3 — Day 3
1. Arjun
2. Aubrey
3. Lacey
4. Anna
5. Liam
6. Mia
7. Amena
8. Cian

Week 3 — Day 4
1. 10
2. 7
3. 9
4. 8
5. 9
6. 15
7. 14
8. 18
9. 16
10. 19

Week 3 — Day 5
1. 1
2. 3
3. 6
4. 5
5. 10
6. 7
7. 9
8. 13

Week 4 — Day 1
1. 8
2. 4
3. 10
4. 16
5. 27
6. 45
7. 12
8. 20
9. 38
10. 50

Week 4 — Day 2
1. yes
2. no
3. yes
4. no
5. no
6. yes
7. no
8. yes
9. yes
10. yes

Week 4 — Day 3
1. 10, 15
2. 25, 30
3. 35, 40
4. 30, 35
5. 45, 50
6. 40, 45
7. 5, 10
8. 20, 25

Week 4 — Day 4
1. 9 + 1
2. 12 − 2
3. 7 + 3
4. 11 − 1
5. 15 − 5
6. 8 + 2
7. 19 − 9
8. 13 − 3
9. 6 + 4
10. 18 − 8

Week 4 — Day 5
1. Jack says: 30
   June says: 5, 30
2. Jack says: 10
   June says: 15, 10
3. Jack says: 40
   June says: 40, 25
4. Jack says: 50
   June says: 50, 45

Week 5 — Day 1
1. 14, 18
2. 19, 13
3. 16, 11
4. 9, 20
5. 17, 10

Week 5 — Day 2
1. 9
2. 15
3. 7
4. 14
5. 15
6. 8
7. 17
8. 14
9. 0
10. 20

Week 5 — Day 3
1. 4 − 1 = 3
2. 10 − 3 = 7
3. 8 − 4 = 4
4. 12 − 0 = 12
5. 20 − 1 = 19
6. 15 − 4 = 11
7. 17 − 5 = 12
8. 14 − 5 = 9

Week 5 — Day 4
1. 1
2. 3
3. 5
4. 2
5. 6
6. 2
7. 6
8. 9

Week 5 — Day 5
1. 4
2. 10
3. 8
4. 6
5. 16
6. 20
7. 14

Week 6 — Day 1
1. 2 is less than 6.
2. 7 is less than 9.
3. 16 is more than 6.
4. 15 is more than 7.
5. 11 is less than 19.
6. 12 is more than 8.
7. 5 is more than 4.
8. 6 is less than 8.
9. 11 is less than 13.
10. 17 is less than 18.

Week 6 — Day 2
1. 15, 14
2. 32, 31
3. 19, 18
4. 47, 46
5. 40, 39

Week 6 — Day 3
1. 2 + 1 = 3
2. 10 − 2 = 8
3. 7 + 3 = 10
4. 9 + 2 = 11
5. 14 + 4 = 18
6. 15 − 5 = 10
7. 8 + 6 = 14
8. 7 − 4 = 3
9. 11 + 4 = 15
10. 18 − 2 = 16

Week 6 — Day 4
1. 10, 20
2. 30, 40
3. 20, 25
4. 5, 15
5. 25, 35

Week 6 — Day 5
1. 2, 5
2. 7, 3
3. 4, 5
4. 3, 12
5. 3, 5

Week 7 — Day 1
1. 18, 16
2. 24, 22
3. 12, 10
4. 40, 38
5. 47, 45
6. 53, 51
7. 69, 67
8. 41, 39
9. 76, 74
10. 71, 69

Week 7 — Day 2
1. 5 cm
2. 3 cm
3. 6 cm
4. 2 cm
5. 9 cm

Week 7 — Day 3
1. 6
2. 12
3. 7
4. 16
5. 9
6. 15
7. 2
8. 20
9. 11
10. 19

Week 7 — Day 4
1. 5 + 4 = 9
2. 3 + 10 = 13
3. 6 + 6 = 12
4. 13 + 5 = 18
5. 3 + 8 = 11
6. 8 + 12 = 20
7. 6 + 7 = 13
8. 9 + 8 = 17

Week 7 — Day 5
1. 4
2. 2
3. 3
4. 7
5. 9
6. 10
7. 17
8. 7
9. 8
10. 5

Week 8 — Day 1
1. 15 − 7 = **8**
2. 0 + 11 = **11**
3. 12 − 8 = **4**
4. 17 − 0 = **17**
5. 6 + 13 = **19**

Week 8 — Day 2
1. 50 grams, heavier
2. 10 grams, lighter
3. 20 grams, lighter
4. 40 grams, heavier

Week 8 — Day 3
1. 3
2. 4
3. 5
4. 4
5. 3
6. 4
7. 6
8. 5
9. 6
10. 8

Week 8 — Day 4
1. 11, 12
2. 26, 30
3. 20, 40
4. 35, 40
5. 15, 14

Week 8 — Day 5
1. 7
2. 10
3. 6
4. 9
5. 8
6. 12
7. 14
8. 16
9. 15
10. 13

Week 9 — Day 1
The numbers that should be crossed out are:
1. 34, 19
2. 44
3. 17, 24
4. 8, 49
5. 6, 19, 26
6. 16, 54, 22
7. 4, 21
8. 28
9. 14, 18, 24
10. 43, 39

Week 9 — Day 2
1. 11
2. 6
3. 10
4. 16
5. 8
6. 7
7. 1
8. 0
9. 3
10. 5

Week 9 — Day 3
1. yes
2. no
3. yes
4. yes
5. yes
6. no
7. no
8. yes
9. yes
10. no

Week 9 — Day 4
1.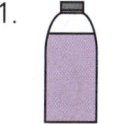
2.
3.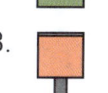
4.
5.
6.
7.
8.

Week 9 — Day 5
1. 3p
2. 11p
3. 7p
4. 4p
5. 11p
6. 25p
7. 16p
8. 27p

Week 10 — Day 1
1. 14, 13
2. 31, 29
3. 1, 0
4. 49, 48
5. 41, 39

Week 10 — Day 2
1. 10
2. 8
3. 9
4. 17
5. 20
6. 16
7. 12
8. 19
9. 11
10. 15

Week 10 — Day 3
1.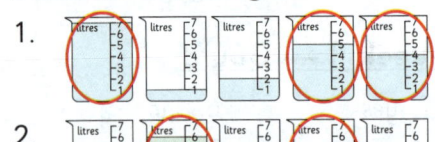
2.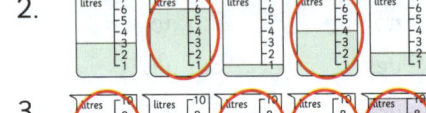
3.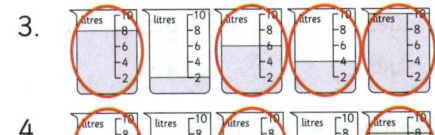
4.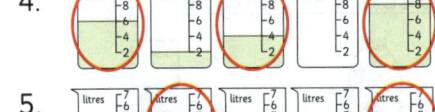
5.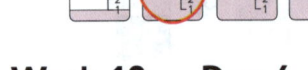

Week 10 — Day 4
1. 35
2. 24
3. 15
4. 60
5. 9
6. 19
7. 1
8. 17
9. 11
10. 17

Week 10 — Day 5
1. 1
2. 4
3. 5
4. 11
5. 15
6. 12
7. 9
8. 8

Week 11 — Day 1
1. six
2. nine
3. seventeen
4. ten
5. thirteen
6. eleven
7. fourteen
8. eighteen
9. twelve
10. sixteen

Week 11 — Day 2
1. ✗
2. ✓
3. ✓
4. ✗
5. ✗
6. ✓
7. ✗
8. ✓
9. ✗
10. ✓

Week 11 — Day 3
1. 4
2. 10
3. 16
4. 14
5. 12
6. 3
7. 5
8. 8
9. 13
10. 7

Week 11 — Day 4
1. 2
2. 3
3. 4
4. 5
5. 6
6. 7

Week 11 — Day 5
1. 11
2. 14
3. 8
4. 20
5. 6
6. 19

Week 12 — Day 1
1. ✓
2. ✗
3. ✓
4. ✓
5. ✗
6. ✓
7. ✗
8. ✓

Week 12 — Day 2
1. 6
2. 14, 18
3. 32, 38
4. 22
5. 8, 12
6. 18, 20, 24
7. 26
8. 36, 40
9. 30, 36
10. 42, 48

Week 12 — Day 3
1. 4
2. 8
3. 7
4. 4
5. 3
6. 7
7. 6
8. 13
9. 3
10. 7

Week 12 — Day 4
1. 6 litres
2. 4 litres
3. 5 litres
4. 7 litres
5. 10 litres
6. 14 litres
7. 6 litres
8. 8 litres
9. 10 litres
10. 12 litres

Week 12 — Day 5
1. 2
2. 7
3. 3
4. 6
5. 4
6. 5
7. 8
8. 7